20TH CENTURY ART
1980-2000
VERY modern art
A HISTORY OF MODERN ART

Clare Oliver

Heinemann
LIBRARY

CONTENTS

ART STYLES...& STARS
5
WORLDS OF WORDS
6
EXPLORING EMPTINESS
8
ABSTRACT COLOURS
10
PAINT & EMOTION
12
BAD PAINTING
14
GRAFFITI ART
16
BIG SCULPTURE
18
STRANGE MATERIALS
20
KITSCH IS COOL
22
CAUGHT ON CAMERA
24
VIDEO ART
26
COMPUTER-AGE ART
28
GLOSSARY & TIMELINE
30
INDEX
32

FALL OF THE BERLIN WALL
During the '80s and '90s, the so-called Iron Curtain was slowly lifted. The USSR split up, and Berlin became a single city once more, with the fall of its Wall in '89.

VIDEO ART
Many artists chose video as their medium. Nam June Paik, credited with creating the first video art in the '60s, continued to make thought-provoking multi-monitor installations.

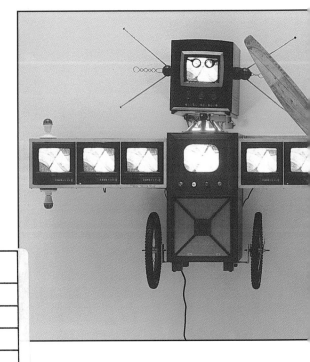

ART STYLES...& STARS

The last two decades of the 20th century saw the acceptance of 'new' media for art, including photography, video and digital art. The computer revolution finally arrived in the mid-1980s, when the Internet opened up to public access.

Meanwhile, the old art forms were not dead. Sculpture was well-supported – the financial boom of the '80s meant more commissions for sculptors. Painting, neglected during the '60s and '70s, reappeared with the emotional works of the Neo-Expressionists and Graffiti artists.

These movements gave rise to the biggest art stars since Andy Warhol – Julian Schnabel and Jean-Michel Basquiat. It was a time of big names. Next came Jeff Koons and then, in the '90s, the focus switched to London as Damien Hirst shocked the world with displays of pickled animals. As the 21st century dawned, it seemed that the boundaries of art were being pushed further than ever before.

HIGH TECH ALLERGY (DETAIL), *Nam June Paik, 1995*

VIRTUAL STARS
Toy Story ('95) made cinematic history as the first full-length feature produced entirely on computer. Previously, movie-goers had only seen short bursts of computer-generated special effects.

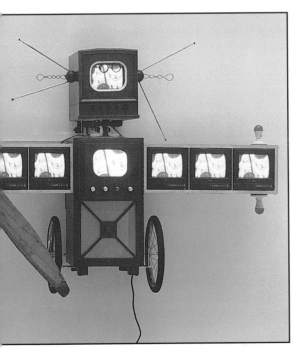

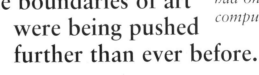

DIGITAL REVOLUTION
There were huge leaps forward in technology, and Microsoft founder Bill Gates (right) made millions.

WORLDS OF WORDS

Since the 1960s, Conceptual artists have incorporated words in their art as part of their explorations into the nature of 'meaning'.

WORD ASSOCIATION

American artist Bruce Nauman (*b.* 1941) has worked in different media over the last four decades, including Performance and Video Art, but most people know

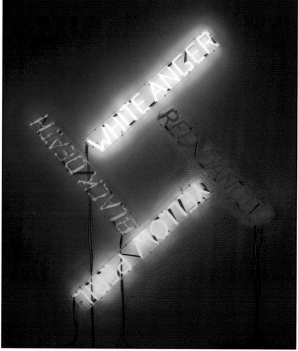

WHITE ANGER/RED DANGER/YELLOW PERIL/ BLACK DEATH, *Bruce Nauman, 1985*

him for his neon 'word' sculptures. The words are thought-provoking and can seem to sum up the nature of existence – phrases in his *One Hundred Live and Die* ('94) include 'Rage and Die' and 'Think and Live.' The phrases

PAIRED TO PROVOKE
Here, the word pairings for 'Red', 'White and 'Black' seem obvious, inoffensive word associations. But when Nauman combines 'Yellow' with 'Peril', it makes an unpleasant nickname that was used in the past to refer to the Chinese. So in this sculpture, Nauman exposes and attacks people's deep-rooted racism.

Scruffy Kurt Cobain (1967–94) fronted Nirvana, the biggest-selling grunge band.

GENERATION GRUNGE
In his book *Generation X*, Douglas Coupland identified the 'slacker' generation. He argued that in the '90s there was nothing left to fight for. Instead, angst-ridden young people were embracing a directionless life. This could be seen in grunge music, which was often about being bored. Movies such as *Slacker* and *Clerks* also depicted youngsters who'd opted out of the rat race.

often read like word association tests, too. These tests are designed to help diagnose mental illness by tapping into a patient's deepest thoughts. The patient has to respond to a word or picture by saying the first thing that comes to mind.

ALL IN THE MIND

New York artist Sean Landers (*b.* 1962) also uses words that seem to pour from the subconscious, or inner mind. With a very small brush, he fills the canvas with poems – strings of tiny words. Landers explains 'See I wanted to paint pictures but I wasn't that great at it so I decided to write on them to make them better. And check it out, it worked!'

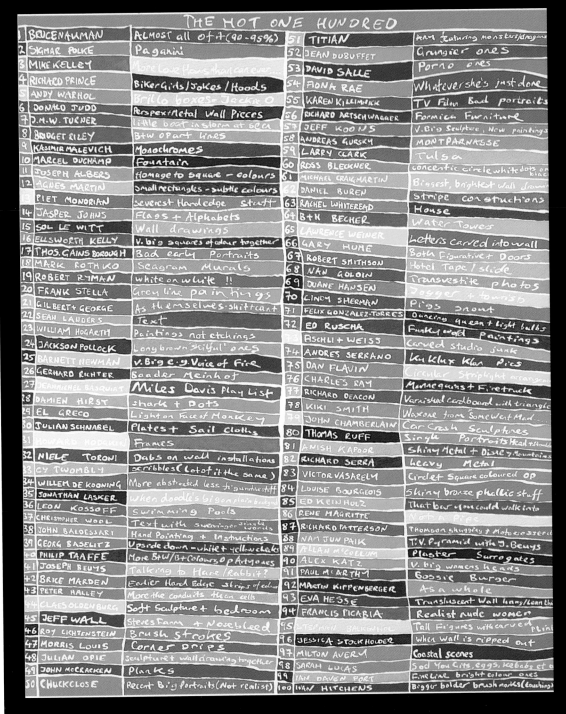

THE HOT ONE HUNDRED
PETER DAVIES, 1997

Davies is known for his 'artist league tables'. In each new 'list', the artists change position – by the time of *The Hip One Hundred* ('98), for example, Bruce Nauman had dropped eight places to No. 9. Davies said his opinions change even as he makes a painting, so he does not agree with the order by the time a painting is finished. This is Davies' way of showing how short-lived celebrity can be, as well as how ideas change and evolve over time. Davies is also exposing how influential fashion is in the art world, and in the way people look at art.

SLACKER SEAN

Often, the words in Landers' pieces are spelt wrong, and the ideas can also seem rather childish. He has come to stand for the 'slacker generation' – the '90s youth known for their despairing lack of ambition. Still, Landers himself is a big success.

IN AT NO. 1

Landers was No. 1 in *Text-Painting* ('96) by Peter Davies (*b.* 1970) – a list of artists whom Davies liked. Landers responded by painting: 'Hey English guy whose copying my work and nameing me as the greatest artist. Thanks and youre right but youre eating into my profits.'

EXPLORING EMPTINESS

Minimalist sculptures are simple forms. They allow artists to explore concepts of time, space and sound. One of the strangest effects is a sense of emptiness.

INSIDE OUT

Rachel Whiteread (*b.* 1963) is famous for her casts of negative spaces, such as the area under a bed. This idea was not completely new – Bruce Nauman made a cast of the space under his chair in the '60s. In '93, Whiteread won the Turner Prize for *House*, a cast of the interior of an entire house that was due for demolition. This huge, short-lived sculpture captured the memories and lives of people who once lived in the house. For the Holocaust Memorial in Vienna, Whiteread created *Untitled (Book Corridors)* ('98), a cast of the inside of a destroyed library. The concave spines of thousands of books commemorated the 65,000 Austrian Jews who died in the World War II Holocaust.

8

AT THE EDGE OF THE WORLD
ANISH KAPOOR, 1998

Bombay-born Anish Kapoor (*b.* 1954) makes massive, mystical sculptures. He is interested in the void, which he calls the 'in-between space'. He represents this through forms with deep hollows. Looking up into *At the Edge of the World* is a disorientating experience. It is impossible to tell where the cavity ends. By creating supreme emptiness, Kapoor also gives the viewer a sense of infinity. Similarly, when the viewer looks into the back of one of Kapoor's empty blue half-spheres, the back is dark, invisible and difficult to grasp. However, if the viewer makes a noise, the sculpture amplifies the sound, to give a suggestion of the space.

HOUSE, Rachel Whiteread, 1993

BREAKING DOWN WALLS
Rachel Whiteread (right) created this inverted sculpture of a house in Bow, London. It was demolished on January 11, '94.

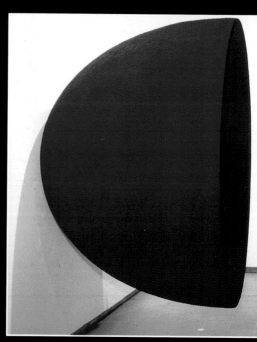

UNTITLED, *Anish Kapoor, 1990*

Anish Kapoor

IS THERE ANYTHING THERE?

Some of Kapoor's works are coloured by a bright, powdery pigment. Others are cast in shiny, reflective metal or carved in stone. They all play with ideas of space, blurring the boundaries between visible and invisible. *When I Am Pregnant* ('92), for example, is a white bulge that projects from the gallery wall. It can only be seen from the side – when the viewer stands face-on, the wall appears flat!

ABSTRACT COLOURS

Abstract art focuses on form and colour instead of trying to depict scenes realistically. Its first wave of popularity was around 1910–20 and it has remained a key part of the art scene ever since.

ABSTRACT LANDSCAPES

Even the most Abstract art can be based on inspiration from nature. In the '80s, British artist Bridget Riley (*b.* 1931) produced large oil paintings of coloured vertical stripes, such as *Burnished Sky* ('85), and then 'diagonal' paintings of distorted diamonds, such as *Certain Day* ('89). Behind each work is a grid, but despite this mathematical precision, the paintings all suggest landscape, and not just because of their titles. This is partly due to Riley's palette – known for her black and white acrylics in the '60s, she now employs earthy oranges, pinks and reds along with sky blues and grassy greens.

COLOURED SHAPES
Painter Patrick Heron (above) was also an art critic and often wrote about colour theory. His art hero of the past was Henri Matisse (1869–1954), whose last works were collages of cut-out coloured paper shapes.

Hirst poses in front of a dot painting at the '95 Turner Prize ceremony.

DOTTY DAMIEN
Best known for sharks or cows in formaldehyde, Damien Hirst also produces paintings. His two key styles of the '90s were 'dot' paintings (above), such as *Carbon Monoxide* ('96), and 'spin' paintings (made by spinning paint on to the canvas). The actual pictures are made by assistants.

TAKEN FROM NATURE

British artist Patrick Heron (1920–99) was part of the St. Ives School that flourished in the '50s and '60s. The Cornish landscape inspired his paintings, but they became increasingly abstract – it can be hard to make out a recognisable rock or tree among the bold or scribbly shapes. Heron believed that all painting was abstract, but even so it made 'the outside world visible', or at least, the artist's view of it. He thought beauty was to be found in a painting's rhythm – the way the different parts of it led the viewer's eye and related to each other. 'The subject matter of a painting is the least important thing', he said.

ST. JOHN
GERHARD RICHTER, 1988

St. John is one of Richter's 'London Paintings', abstract works in oil inspired by trips to the chapels at Westminster Abbey in London. Many of Richter's works look rather like the Impressionist paintings of French artist Claude Monet (1840–1926). As in Monet's famous 'Waterlilies' series, Richter's colours merge and wobble like watery reflections. Also, the works of both artists feature layers of thick colour that make a built-up, textured surface. But Monet was trying to represent his impression of the landscape, whereas Richter insists that he is not trying to show the external world at all. In *St. John* and the other 'London Paintings', Richter is trying to show how being in St. John's Chapel made him *feel*, not what it looked like.

COMMON INSPIRATIONS...MANY STYLES

Heron admired Henri Matisse (1869–1954), one of the first artists to explore abstraction. Matisse wanted to make restful works, 'like a good armchair'. Matisse also inspired David Hockney (*b.* 1937), whose recent abstracts feature bright, joyful shapes. Hockney does not only make abstract works – his other styles include photomontage. Similarly, German artist Gerhard Richter (*b.* 1932) switches between photo-realistic painting and *Abstraktes Bild* (abstract painting).

ONE STYLE OF MANY
British artist David Hockney shot to fame in the '60s with his Pop paintings of swimming pools and decadent living. His works in the '90s included explorations of abstraction, inspired by Matisse.

PAINT & EMOTION

In the 1980s there was new interest in painting after the dominance of theory-based installation and sculpture during the '60s and '70s. In '81 London's Royal Academy put on 'A New Spirit in Painting', an exhibition of large, intense works from all over Europe.

THE TRANSAVANTGARDE

In Italy, this new, emotional movement in painting was called the Transavantgarde. The key artists were Sandro Chia (*b.* 1946), Enzo Cucchi (*b.* 1949), Francesco Clemente (*b.* 1952) and Mimmo Paladino (*b.* 1948). All four produced expressive figure work, but each in his own particular style. Chia fills every centimetre of the canvas with paint, while Cucchi's works can be sparse but mystical. Clemente and Paladino produce dark, frightening pieces – a huge, untitled work by Clemente in '83, for example, shows a head with other heads escaping from the eye sockets, mouth, nostrils and ear.

Revellers celebrated in '89 by pulling down the Berlin Wall.

THE WALL FALLS

German painters often used their art to work through feelings about their country's recent history, especially the Nazi atrocities before and during World War II. On its defeat in '45, Germany had been split to make two separate states. Berlin was half in East and half in West Germany, with the two sides kept separate by the Berlin Wall. Germany finally became a single country again in '89.

CHIA IN HIS STUDIO
Sandro Chia (below in '91) is a very prolific artist. His figures often appear in heroic or classical poses. His style of painting is more colourful and not as gloomy as that of his contemporaries.

LILITH
ANSELM KIEFER, 1987-89

Kiefer painted *Lilith* after a trip to Sao Paulo, Brazil. Lilith is a mythological figure of evil – the Babylonians knew her as Lilit, ghost of desolate places. Kiefer shows Sao Paulo as a desolate place. He mixed ash into the oil paint to show the filth and pollution produced by industry. He added chaotic copper wire at the bottom of the picture to show how communication had become scrambled.

THE NEO-EXPRESSIONISTS

In Germany, the new use of heavy blobs and smears of paint was the perfect way to express emotions about German history. Known as the Neo-Expressionists, German artists included A.R. Penck (*b.* 1939) and Georg Baselitz (*b.* 1938), who can both remember the bombing of Dresden. Baselitz's work is gloomy and unsettling and he often gives his people huge, blank eyes.

DEATH AND DESTRUCTION

Younger Neo-Expressionists include Markus Lüpertz (*b.* 1941), Anselm Kiefer (*b.* 1945) and Rainer Fetting (*b.* 1949). Death and decay dominate Kiefer's paintings, which are often based on violent mythological stories. Kiefer is famous for mixing organic materials with his paint, such as straw, that will eventually decompose. Sometimes, his canvases feature lead or copper, which also change over time as they oxidise and corrode in the air.

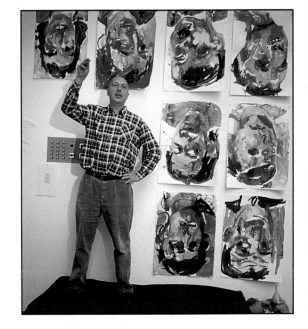

TURNING ART ON ITS HEAD
Since '69, Baselitz (above) has hung his splodgy paintings upside-down. He actually paints them the wrong way up, too. This forces the viewer really to experience the surface of the piece, with its thick paint, rather than concentrating just on the image.

BAD PAINTING

Neo-Expressionism also appeared in the USA. There, the rough, crude style was used as a symbol of the poverty of civilisation as a whole. This led to the term 'Bad Painting' and some critics wrote-off the new generation as too slapdash and raw. Others, however, discovered some Bad Painting was *good*!

President Reagan with British Prime Minister Margaret Thatcher, who shared his economic ideas.

THE REAGAN YEARS

Ronald Reagan was the US President from '81 until '89. He believed in the free market and cut taxes dramatically while he was in power. Until the worldwide stock market crash of '87, this fostered a boom. Wages rose and people had more cash to spend on luxury goods, including art, which fetched record-breaking prices.

MATERIALS WITH MEANING

The biggest star in the US art scene of the early '80s was Julian Schnabel (*b*. 1951). He shot to fame for his 'plate paintings', which were a kind of collage. They had stuck-on pieces of crockery and thick, gloopy paint applied under and over them.

Schnabel left some plates whole, but others were smashed, so that their sharp edges stuck out of the picture. The excess of dull-coloured paint seemed to be a perfect symbol for the ugly excesses in the '80s' climate of greed, while the broken shards of pottery reflected society's violence and aggression. 'I wanted to make something that was exploding as much as I wanted to make something cohesive' (that hung together), he once explained.

MONEY, MONEY, MONEY Wall Street is New York's financial district and home to the New York and American Stock Exchanges, as well as the Federal Reserve Bank. It was at the heart of the stockbroking boom of the '80s, creating millionaire art enthusiasts.

MIXED MESSAGES

Schnabel recycles old art styles in his work that often conflict with each other. His subject matter is diverse, too, ranging from Norse mythology to recent history. It is as though he wants to show everything in the world all at once in each picture. At the same time, Schnabel's work is deeply personal – his way of making an impression on a fragmented world. 'I want my life to be embedded in my work…crushed into my painting, like a pressed car,' he said.

14

HUMANITY ASLEEP

JULIAN SCHNABEL, 1982

Humanity Asleep is one of Schnabel's plate paintings, embedded with broken crockery. The paint has been applied thickly and crudely, to make a relief (raised surface) effect. It looks rough and ready, almost like a child has made it. This painting is on canvas, but Schnabel has worked on a variety of surfaces, including ponyskin, carpet and velvet.

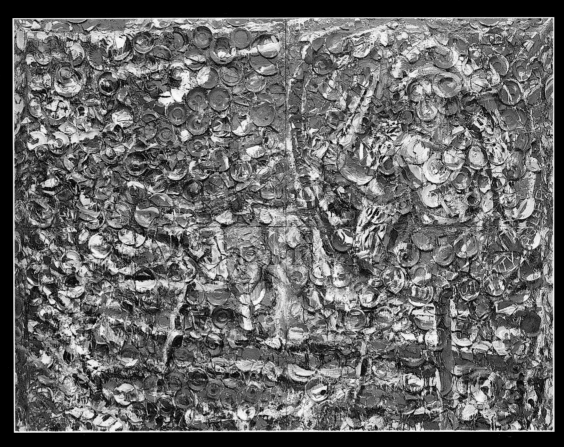

THE HIGH LIFE
Trump Tower, opened in '83, is part of the real-estate empire of multi-millionaire Donald Trump. Every New Yorker who lived the high life rented an apartment there, including gallery owner Jeffrey Deitch, who made a fortune out of the '80s art boom.

WHOSE ART?

For one of his pieces, Schnabel bought a diptych called *Daemonization* ('80) by fellow-American and 'Bad' painter David Salle (*b.* 1952). Schnabel swapped the two panels around and painted a portrait of Salle on top of one of the panels. He signed the painting as his own and titled it *Jump* ('80). In this way, Schnabel raised questions about who the artist of the piece was, and what it could mean. Both Salle and Schnabel used their work to turn traditional ideas about art on their head.

CROCKS OF GOLD
Schnabel used a variety of cheap crockery in his paintings of the early '80s – some patterned and some plain – sticking the pieces on with cement or industrial adhesives. The finished paintings sold for astronomical sums of money.

GRAFFITI ART

Throughout the 1980s, New York remained the capital of the art world. The most exclusively American art movement was Graffiti Art, rooted in the artistic vandalism on the New York Subway. Its key figures were Jean-Michel Basquiat (1960–88) and Keith Haring (1958–90).

16

Basquiat (above in '85) was a snappy dresser and the darling of New York. He wore expensive Armani suits while painting.

ARROZ CON POLLO (RICE AND CHICKEN)
JEAN-MICHEL BASQUIAT, 1981

Basquiat's work first appeared on walls and often featured scrawled-on writing or symbols, but he claimed 'My work has nothing to do with graffiti. It is painting and it always has been.' Exploring the 'black' experience, Basquiat drew on African, Puerto Rican and Haitian imagery, such as fetishes, crucifixes, skulls and totems. In this painting, named after a Carribean dish, the figure on the left resembles a devil or a Voodoo doll stuck with pins.

ON THE WALL
Keith Haring painted many murals in New York, such as Crack is Wack *(right, '87). Crack cocaine, a highly-addictive drug, became an increasing problem during the '80s. The message of Haring's wall painting was that drug-taking was bad ('wack').*

CARTOONS WITH A MESSAGE

Haring's cartoony style is instantly recognisable, with its thick black outlines and stylised figures. Popular on greetings cards and teeshirts, it was also put to serious use, for example in the fight against drug abuse. In *Ignorance=Fear* ('89), Haring reinterpreted the Three Monkeys (See No Evil, Hear No Evil and Speak No Evil) for an AIDS awareness poster.

IN THE END

Both Haring and Basquiat died tragically young – Haring of AIDS and Basquiat of a heroin overdose. After Basquiat's death, painter Julian Schnabel made a film about his life.

FEAR AND IGNORANCE
AIDS (Acquired Immune Deficiency Syndrome) is a terrible disease that destroys the body's natural defences. HIV, the virus that causes it, was identified in '83. At first, there was a great deal of ignorance about AIDS – tabloids dubbed it the 'gay plague', for example. Charity groups such as ACT UP in the USA and the Terence Higgins Trust in Britain had to campaign hard to raise awareness.

British artists Gilbert & George stand before their picture Bleeding *at an AIDS charity event in May '89.*

BIG SCULPTURE

Large-scale sculptures and installations, which had become popular during the 1960s and '70s, continued to appear, and established artists from those decades carried on making new work.

OLD STYLES REVISITED

Pop artist Roy Lichtenstein (1923–97) carried on his cartoon-style work, with large painted metal sculptures of three-dimensional brushstrokes such as *Mural with Blue Brushstrokes* ('86) in New York. Claes Oldenburg (*b.* 1929) and Coosje van Bruggen (*b.* 1942) also created mammoth Pop sculptures, such as their outsized needle and thread in Milan, Italy (2000). Christo (*b.* 1935) and Jeanne-Claude (*b.* 1935) continued with their environmental work, famously wrapping the German parliament, the Reichstag, in '95.

*ANARCHY IN THE GALLERY
Horn's* Concert for Anarchy *('90) features a grand piano that bursts open above the viewer's head. Horn says 'The tragic and melancholic aspect of machines is very important to me.'*

MICRO SCULPTURES

At the same time as artists were creating large-scale works, Willard Wigan began to make record-breakingly tiny sculptures!

BOXING RING, *Willard Wigan*

MACHINES GONE MAD

Large-scale works can create a sense of unease and dislocation – they take things out of context and force the viewer to look at them with new eyes. For this reason, they appeal to feminist artists, who want to show how society excludes women. German artist Rebecca Horn (*b.* 1944) makes disturbing mechanical sculptures. In works such as *Concert for Anarchy* ('90), Horn quite literally turns traditional, male culture (represented by a grand piano) on its head. The work suggests the idea of hanging on to sanity by a thread – and threatens imminent violence if it snaps.

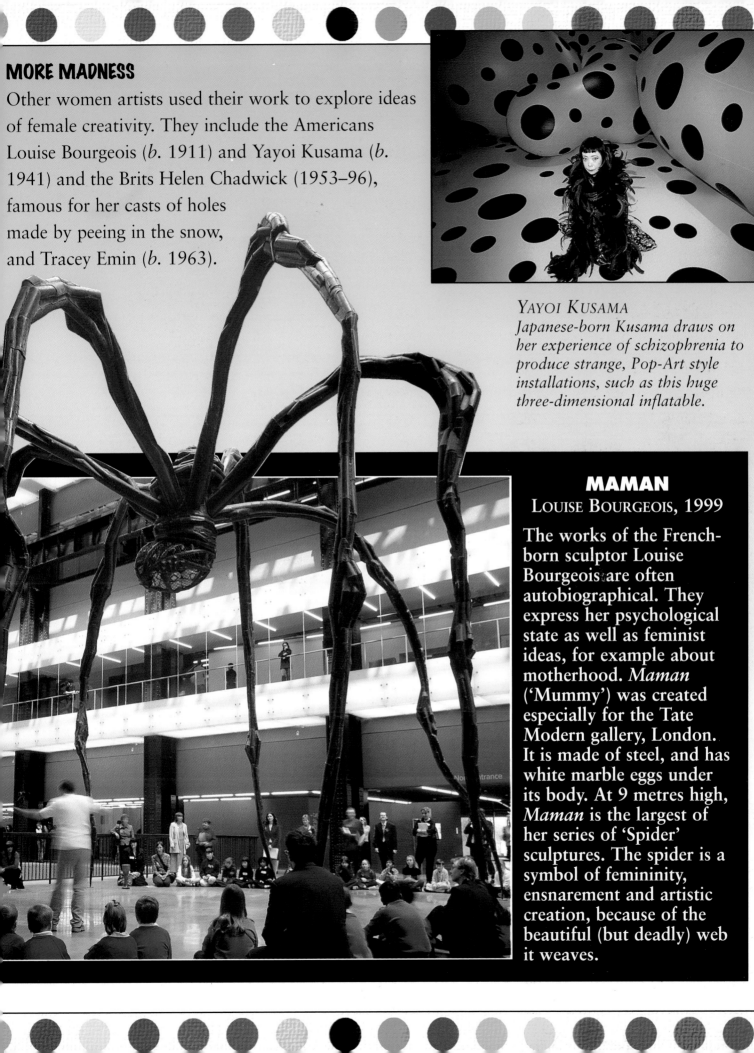

MORE MADNESS

Other women artists used their work to explore ideas of female creativity. They include the Americans Louise Bourgeois (*b.* 1911) and Yayoi Kusama (*b.* 1941) and the Brits Helen Chadwick (1953–96), famous for her casts of holes made by peeing in the snow, and Tracey Emin (*b.* 1963).

YAYOI KUSAMA
Japanese-born Kusama draws on her experience of schizophrenia to produce strange, Pop-Art style installations, such as this huge three-dimensional inflatable.

MAMAN
LOUISE BOURGEOIS, 1999

The works of the French-born sculptor Louise Bourgeois are often autobiographical. They express her psychological state as well as feminist ideas, for example about motherhood. *Maman* ('Mummy') was created especially for the Tate Modern gallery, London. It is made of steel, and has white marble eggs under its body. At 9 metres high, *Maman* is the largest of her series of 'Spider' sculptures. The spider is a symbol of femininity, ensnarement and artistic creation, because of the beautiful (but deadly) web it weaves.

19

STRANGE MATERIALS

The desire to shock or provoke has led many artists to experiment with new, unusual materials in their art.

ANIMAL MAGIC

Damien Hirst (*b.* 1965) works in many different media. His work includes wall pieces – shelves that display collections of objects, such as seashells or surgical instruments. However, he is best-known for his vitrines (glass tanks) containing animals or fish preserved in formaldehyde. In *Mother and Child Divided* ('93), for example, he showed a bisected (cut in two) cow and calf.

USEFUL DUNG
Ofili (above) uses balls of dung in his art and also as stands to display the finished pieces.

ELEPHANT DUNG

Fellow-Brit Chris Ofili (*b.* 1968) creates beautiful, decorative works in lush colours. He often makes collages, using magazine cuttings, sequins, dreadlocks (hair) and, controversially, small balls of elephant dung! Ofili explains 'I made a decision to make these paintings that were really ornate and…I wanted to include something in the paintings that would criticise that – to challenge that.' It is Ofili's way of anticipating being pigeon-holed as a black artist. He does not want his blackness to be treated as exotic and ethnic – the dung demonstrates that not everything from Africa is exotic!

THE PHYSICAL IMPOSSIBILITY OF DEATH IN THE MIND OF SOMEONE LIVING
DAMIEN HIRST, 1991

Hirst's most notorious vitrine work displayed a dead tiger shark. Most people refer to the work as *Shark*, but its real title gives us a clue about what the piece means. Sharks are nature's supreme killing machines, but here, the viewer sees how all living things ultimately die. The piece also explores how living things are displayed in museums, where they become lifeless objects taken out of their natural environments. Finally, of course, it is a fascinating experience to be able to see a scary shark in close-up – and as an object of beauty rather than fear.

Damien Hirst is the best-known British artist of his generation.

OFILI IN AFRICA

Chris Ofili was born in Manchester but his parents were originally from Nigeria, West Africa. Ofili's first-hand experience of Africa came on a scholarship to Zimbabwe in '92. There he came across the ancient dot paintings on cave walls made by the Matopos – their decorative style inspired his work. Ofili is also fascinated by the body scarring practised by the Nuba people in Sudan, East Africa. Decorating the body in this way is a religious ritual and an art form. It often marks momentous events in a person's life, such as coming of age.

A young Nuba endures the painful ritual of body scarring.

BLOODY ART

Another British artist, Marc Quinn (*b*. 1964), rose to fame by using blood – his own! *Self* ('91) is a unique self-portrait – a sculpture of Quinn's head that has to be stored in a fridge because it is made out of 4.5 litres of his frozen blood. It was a continuation of the Body Art first popular in the '60s.

KITSCH IS COOL

During the 1960s, Pop artists had taken shallow subject matter from popular culture – reacting against the supercharged emotion of the Abstract Expressionists. In the '80s, a new generation of artists drew inspiration from tacky goods. Was this cynical, empty art or a cool comment on greed and capitalism?

TRASH CULTURE

Jean-Paul Gaultier is the fashion designer who put men in skirts and pop star Madonna in an over-the-top bustier. He also co-presented *Eurotrash*, a TV show of Kitsch clips from across Europe. French artists Pierre et Gilles made a sentimental portrait of Gaultier (*Jean Paul*, '90) surrounded by daisies.

Fashion designer Jean-Paul Gaultier co-presented cult TV show Eurotrash.

SCHLOCK HORROR!

The new style was called Kitsch or Schlock, meaning trashy, sugary and sentimental. It commonly included cute little animals or flowers. Religious icons are another good source for Kitsch. French artists Pierre et Gilles (*f.* 1977) photograph famous stars – including Boy George, Paloma Picasso and Catherine Deneuve – looking like Christian saints, figures from Greek myth, or Hindu gods.

SENTIMENTAL SAINT Originally, Kitsch copied gift shop tack, but then, shops were inspired by Kitsch! There was a market for fun objects that were deliberately in bad taste – like this glow-in-the-dark St. Clare!

KITSCH KOONS

The most successful Kitsch artist is Jeff Koons (*b.* 1955), who began by putting ordinary objects, such as vacuum cleaners or basketballs, in perspex cases like museum displays. Next, he made replicas of tasteless souvenirs.

PRETTY PUPPY

Koons' *Puppy* ('97) stands in front of the Guggenheim Museum in Bilbao, Spain. The 12.5-metre-high West Highland terrier is made from 60,000 live pansies! It was inspired by a pottery pup Koons saw in a gift shop. He says he made *Puppy* to 'give people a sense of warmth'.

22

POPPLES

JEFF KOONS, 1988

Popples comes from Koons' fourth series of work, known as 'Statuary' – other pieces include *Amore* ('88), a cutesy bear in a bib and nappy. The sculptures are all porcelain copies of real soft toys. Koons is making the meaningless monumental, and forcing the viewer to look closely at trivial, sentimental objects and think about ideas of beauty and taste. Koons, who used to be a Wall Street broker, always claims he is not being snide about banality – 'I don't find any ironic quality in the work at all', he says. In fact, the overwhelming sense is that the objects are being celebrated and enjoyed for what they are. The fun is most evident in *Balloon Dog* ('95), a big, shiny metal sculpture that looks exactly like the balloon animals that children's entertainers make at birthday parties.

Like Pop artist Andy Warhol, Jeff Koons does not make the pieces himself. His role as an artist is choosing the objects and deciding how they will look.

23

CAUGHT ON CAMERA

Since its dawn in the 19th century, photography was considered by many to be Art's poor cousin. Increasingly, however, critics have been forced to recognise the creativity and control demanded by the camera, as artists have pushed photography to the limit.

THE CAMERA NEVER LIES

Some artists use the camera to create scenarios that are far from real. American artist Cindy Sherman (*b.* 1954) has done a series of photographic self-portraits, in which she appears as movie stars or historical figures – in *Untitled #193* ('91), for example, she is an 18th century French lady in a wig! Other artists manipulate their photographs on computer to create fantasy realms – Japanese artist Mariko Mori (*b.* 1967) appears as a cyber-chick in stunning, sci-fi worlds.

MAN AND HORSE JUMPING A FENCE, *Eadweard Muybridge, 1887*

MOVING PICTURES

English photographer Eadweard Muybridge (1830–1904) published his 11-volume *Animal Locomotion* in 1887. Muybridge was one of the first people to see the possibilities of photography. He made his studies of the bodies of people and animals in motion by setting up a row of cameras to go off one by one – using as many as 24 cameras for one sequence.

24

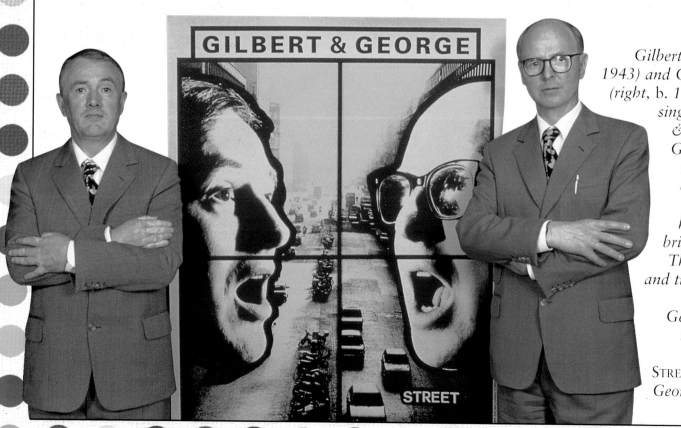

PHOTO PIECES
Gilbert Proesch (left, b. 1943) and George Passmore (right, b. 1942) became the single artist 'Gilbert & George' in '67. Gilbert & George use photographs of men – usually themselves – in huge works with bright, garish tints. The pieces are flat and two-dimensional, but Gilbert & George like to call them sculptures.

STREET, *Gilbert & George, c. 1983*

ABSTRACT ART

German artist Andreas Gursky (*b.* 1955) has used a computer to clean up his images since '92, but the photographs really depend on the strength of his compositions. Typically, Gursky chooses a land- or cityscape which has small, repeated elements, so that it looks almost abstract. 'My preference for clear structures is the result of my desire...to keep track of things and maintain my grip on the world,' he says. Gursky chooses a semi-aerial view so any people are reduced to ant-like figures – for example the workers in *Stock Exchange, Tokyo* ('90) or the people in *Hong Kong, Grand Hyatt Park* ('94).

PEARBLOSSOM HIGHWAY 11–18TH APRIL 1986, *David Hockney, 1986*

MONTAGE MAGIC
British artist Hockney began making photographic 'patchworks' in the '80s. He would stick together hundreds of different snaps to make a landscape.

PARIS, MONTPARNASSE
ANDREAS GURSKY, 1993

This huge – more than 3 metres wide – panorama shows endless rows of miniscule windows on tower blocks along a Parisian street, Montparnasse. The repetition suggests a common Gursky theme – how life in an urban environment is compartmentalised.

Gursky favours a horizontal format for his works, so the viewer's eye darts to and fro across the flat surface, making connections. In the end, the main feature of the work is its sense of a universal order – the pattern that unifies all the tiny, individual elements.

25

VIDEO ART

Throughout the 20th century, artists worked in media that already existed, such as painting and sculpture. But then video exploded on to the scene, and a whole new medium was born.

VERSATILE VIDEO

Video can record Performance Art, tell a story or display abstract images. It can be in a darkened room within a gallery, or projected on to huge public hoardings. It can be shown on a single screen, as in many of the works by Bill Viola (*b.* 1951), including *I Do Not Know What It Is I Am Like* ('86), a film of the artist reflected in an owl's eye. Video Art can also be displayed on many screens at once, as in *Rio Videowall* ('89) by Dara Birnbaum (*b.* 1946). Video walls allow the artist to explore relationships between parts of the image, or compare different images.

26

HIGH TECH ALLERGY
(DETAIL)
NAM JUNE PAIK, 1996

Korean-born Nam June Paik (*b.* 1932) is the father of Video Art – he made the first-ever video piece in '65, when he filmed footage of the Pope's visit to the USA. This is one of a family of 'robots' that Paik has built out of televisions. Paik started out in the '60s as a Performance artist with the experimental Fluxus group – today, his robots are performers in their own right!

Electronic Superhighway was Paik's entry for the Venice Bienniale in '93. He used hundreds of television sets for the work, placing them among lush, tropical plants and objects from popular culture including cars (right). One part of the installation was 'Continental USA' – a gigantic map of the USA made of monitors.

VIDEO SURVEILLANCE

Many video artists explore the ways that television controls people's lives. For her *HIDEO, It's Me, Mama* ('83), Japanese artist Mako Idemitsu (*b.* 1940) created a fictional character called Hideo, whose life is videoed and shown on television. Later, the same idea was behind the Hollywood movie *The Truman Show* ('98). Truman lives happily enough, until he finds out that everyone around him – even his wife – is an actor, and that his life is the plot of an all-day soap opera watched by millions of people.

Actor Jim Carrey played the lead role in The Truman Show *('98).*

ELECTRONIC SUPERHIGHWAY:
BILL CLINTON STOLE MY IDEA (DETAIL)
NAM JUNE PAIK, 1993

STEVE MCQUEEN
In his video work, British artist Steve
McQueen (b. 1966) reacts against the
typical Hollywood stereotypes of black
men. Bear *('93) shows McQueen in a*
boxing match, while in Deadpan *('97) he*
reenacts a scene from an old silent
movie, with himself in the starring role.

VIDEO VIOLENCE

Multiple-channel works give the
artist the chance to juxtapose (put
next to each other) unlikely images.
This can be seen in the chilling
diptych by Swiss artist Pipilotti
Rist, *Ever is Over All* ('97). On
one screen, a smiling woman hums
and walks along the street, but
every so often, she smashes car
windows with a metal, red hot
poker flower. In contrast, the other
screen shows real flowers and the
overall effect is very violent. Twins
Jane and Louise Wilson (*b.* 1967)
also create disturbing video work.
They shoot their films in resonant
locations – *Stasi City* ('97) is set in
the old headquarters of the East
German secret police, and *Gamma
(Silo)* ('99) in the old nuclear
weapons base at Greenham
Common, England.

27

COMPUTER-AGE ART

The very first digital pictures were made in the 1960s by scientists messing about on their machines – they were the only ones with access to a computer, or who could master the long strings of complex commands. But during the '80s, computers became more affordable and user-friendly.

MACHINE-MADE

Early on, the computer's capacity to generate geometric patterns was exploited, but today the opportunities are endless. Of course it is possible to manipulate paintings or photos, but whizzy software has also enabled artists to make three-dimensional objects that only exist onscreen.

BUILDING NEW WORLDS

British artist William Latham (*www.artworks.co.uk*) was one of the first to create virtual 'organisms' – in his *The Evolution of Form* ('90), beautifully patterned three-dimensional creatures mutate and evolve. American Karl Sims (*www.genarts.com/karl*) also investigates evolution, for example in *Galápagos* ('97). His art is interactive, so the viewer can choose environments for the 'organisms'.

MEANWHILE, BACK IN THE (REAL) WORLD...

Digital art has had a far-reaching influence even on artists who do not produce it. Thanks to the Internet, artists no longer have to rely on exhibitions to show their work to the public. Many, including Claes Oldenburg, have home pages that act as permanent galleries. Key in the name of your favourite artist on a search engine and see what you find!

28

THE COOKER
JAKE TILSON, 1994 onwards
www.thecooker.com

British artist Jake Tilson (*b.* 1958) is one of the many web artists who display online. The Internet allows the artist to create multi-layered work that mixes images, text, animation and sound. Often, the work is open-ended, so the viewer navigates around the site by their own choice of links. This means that the artist has no control over the order in which the images or words are encountered! Tilson believes 'You have to allow uncertainty into art. It's that little seep of chaos that creeps in – you have to be ready for it, react to it and let it sit there.' Apart from its ability to reach such an enormous audience, this is one of the most revolutionary aspects of web art. When the 20th century began, the artist was viewed as the controller who presented a completed image to the viewer – web art left the viewer to finish the piece.

PIONEER Completed in '46, ENIAC was one of the very first computers, and as big as a room! By the '80s, the portable laptop was developed.

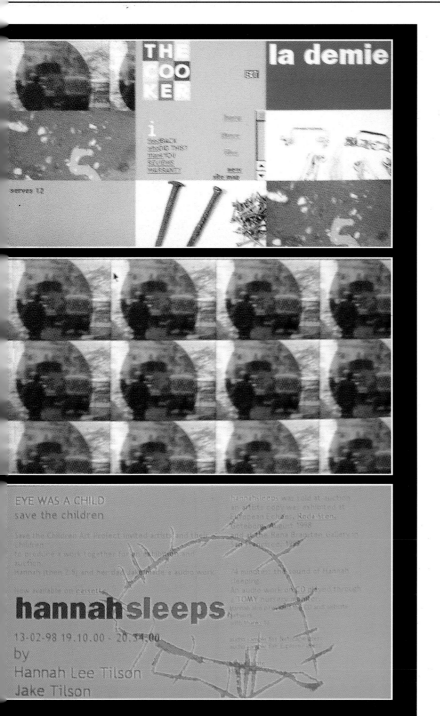

Museum of Modern Art: www.moma.org

The Guggenheim: www.guggenheim.org

The Tate: www.tate.org.uk

ONLINE MUSEUMS & GALLERIES
Major institutions developed their own websites during the '80s and '90s. Visit these ones, or try a web search to discover your own favourites. Most allow you to search their collections and view the art online.

C.G. CINEMA

Computers have revolutionised other art forms. The first full-length computer-generated (C.G.) movie was *Toy Story* ('95). An instant classic, the movie told the tale of rivalry between two toys. But the main attraction was the medium, not the message – the 81 minutes of film had taken the equivalent of 46 continuous days of computer processing.

Buzz Lightyear and Woody were Toy Story's *digital stars.*

GLOSSARY

ABSTRACTION Expressing meaning through shapes and colours, rather than realism.

ABSTRACT EXPRESSIONISM Art style born in the '40s to express emotion through paint and painting techniques.

BAD PAINTING The US Neo-Expressionist movement.

CONCEPTUAL ART Art where the idea is paramount, such as Minimalism or Land Art.

DIPTYCH Artwork presented on a pair of panels, or video art presented on two screens.

FORM The individual shapes in a work of art, and the relationships between them.

FORMALDEHYDE Fluid used to preserve dead bodies.

GRAFFITI ART Art style born in New York in the '80s, inspired by Subway graffiti and often featuring writing.

HOLOCAUST The mass-extermination by the Nazis of Jews and other groups.

IMPRESSIONISM A style from the 1860s, where artists aimed for spontaneous impressions of scenes.

KITSCH Trashy, vulgar or sentimental. Kitsch Art became popular in the '80s.

MINIMALISM An abstract style of art which uses very simple forms or limited colour.

NEO-EXPRESSIONISM A style of painting born in the '80s, marked by its impassioned brushwork and violent energy.

PERFORMANCE ART Art based on theatre, dance, or some other type of performance, often recorded on video.

PIGMENT Coloured paint or dye, or the powder used to colour paint.

POP ART Art style popular from the '50s–'70s that uses the imagery of popular culture.

PHOTO REALISM Art style that records every detail with photographic accuracy.

TRANSAVANTGARDE The Italian Neo-Expressionist movement.

VIDEO ART Art that is presented on video, either on a single screen or on many to make a video wall.

VITRINE A glass tank – *vitrine* is French for 'window'.

WORLD EVENTS

- *Iran-Iraq War begins*
- *Poland: Solidarity set up*   1
- *Egypt: assassination of President Sadat*   1
- *Falklands War between Britain and Argentina*   1
- *HIV virus isolated*   1
- *The Internet opens up to public access*   1
- *Perestroika begins in USSR* •*Ethiopian famine*   1
- *USSR: nuclear accident at Chernobyl*   1
- *Stock markets crash on Black Monday*   1
- *Iran-Iraq War ends* •*Lockerbie air crash*   1
- *Berlin Wall comes down* •*Exxon Valdez oil spill*   1
- *Iraq invades Kuwait: Gulf War breaks out*   1
- *Final break-up of USSR* •*Civil war in Yugoslavia*   1
- *USA: Race riots in L.A.*   1
- *PLO & Israel sign peace agreement*   1
- *Rwanda: Hutus massacre Tutsis*   1
- *Israeli prime minister Yitzhak Rabin assassinated*   1
- •*'Mad Cow' disease – bans on British beef*   1
- *Death of Diana, Princess of Wales*   1
- *Birth of the euro*   1
- *NATO troops in air strikes on Yugoslavia*   1

TIMELINE

	ART	DESIGN	THEATRE & FILM	BOOKS & MUSIC
0	•*Salle:* Daemonization •*Schnabel:* Jump	•*Gae Aulenti: Table With Wheels*	•*John Hurt in* The Elephant Man	•*Anthony Burgess:* Earthly Powers
1	•*R.A., London: 'A New Spirit in Painting' exhib.*	•*Memphis group founded* •*Emporio Armani opens*	•*Gilliam's* Time Bandits •*Dobai & Szabo's* Mephisto	•*Barthes:* Camera Lucida
2	•*Basquiat:* Man from Naples •*Baselitz:* Adieu	•*Tadao Ando: Kidosaki House, Tokyo*	•Bladerunner •E.T. •*Reggio's* Koyaanisqatsi	•*Michael Jackson:* Thriller •*A. Walker:* The Color Purple
3	•*Modena, Italy: 'Transavantguardia' exhib.*	•*Launch of Swatch watch* •*Lagerfeld goes to Chanel*	•*Merce Cunningham dance pieces:* Quartets	•*The Eurythmics:* Sweet Dreams (Are Made of This)
4	•*Braun-Vega:* Fame, after Vermeer…	•*Dyson: G Force bagless vacuum cleaner*	•*Schwarzenegger is* The Terminator •*Amadeus*	•*Kundera:* The Unbearable Lightness of Being
5	•*The Saatchi Gallery opens in London*	•*Michael Graves: Kettle with bird*	•*Harrison Ford in* Witness	•*Don de Lillo:* White Noise •*Kate Bush:* Hounds of Love
6	•*Andreas Schulze:* Portrait of M	•*Richard Rogers' Lloyds Building, London, opens*	•*Berri's* Jean de Florette *and* Manon des Sources	•*Richard Dawkins:* The Blind Watchmaker
7	•*Gober:* Slanted Playpen •*Martin Puryear:* Verge	•*Koolhaas: Netherlands Dance Theatre, The Hague*	•*Richard E. Grant & Paul McGann in* Withnail & I	•*Toni Morrison:* Beloved
8	•*Koons:* Popples •*'Freeze' exhib. of YBAs*	•*I.M. Pei: Grand Louvre Pyramid, Paris*	•*Cartoon characters star in* Who Framed Roger Rabbit?	•*Salman Rushdie:* The Satanic Verses
9	•*Haring:* Ignorance=Fear	•*Nintendo launch GameBoy*	•*Giuseppe Tornatore's* Cinema Paradiso	•*Ayatollah Khomeini issues fatwa against Rushdie*
0	•*Yayoi Kusama:* Mirror Room (Pumpkin)	•*Gaultier designs for Madonna* •*Starck: Juicy Salif*	•*Jeunet & Carot's* Delicatessen •*Edward Scissorhands*	•*Madonna:* The Immaculate Collection
1	•*Marc Quinn:* Self •*Bulatov:* Farewell Lenin	•*Cesar Pelli: Canary Wharf Tower*	•*Richard Linklater's* Slacker •*Thelma and Louise*	•*Coupland:* Generation X •*Nirvana:* Nevermind
2	•*Koons:* Puppy •*Yu Youhan:* Mao and Blonde Girl	•*Gehry: Powerplay chair* •*P. Cox: Wannabe loafers*	•*Disney:* Aladdin •*Tim Robbins in* The Player	•*Brian Eno:* Nerve Net
3	•*Whiteread:* House •*Gursky:* Montparnasse…	•*Hadid: Vitra Fire Station, Weil Am Rhein, Germany*	•*T. Burton's* The Nightmare Before Christmas	•*Nyman:* The Piano •*Björk:* Debut
4	•*Hirst:* Away from the Flock •*Lucas:* Au Naturel	•*Alessi: Anna G corkscrew* •*Versace: safety-pin dress*	•*Paris: Yasmina Reza's* Art •*Tarantino's* Pulp Fiction	•*Portishead:* Dummy •*Irvine Welsh:* Trainspotting
5	•*Goldin:* I'll Be Your Mirror •*M. Barney:* Cremaster I	•*Piano: Kansai International Airport, Osaka, Japan*	•*M. Bourne choreographs* Swan Lake *with male swans*	•*Roth:* Sabbath's Theater •*Pullman:* Northern Lights
6	•*Andreas Gursky:* Hong Kong, Grand Hyatt Park	•*Launch of Sony's PlayStation*	•*Disney:* Toy Story •*T. Burton's* Mars Attacks!	•*Melvin Burgess:* Junk •*John Pawson:* Minimum
7	•*J.& L.Wilson:* Stasi City •*Rist:* Ever Is Over All	•*Ron Arad: Fantastic Plastic Elastic chair*	•*Bowie plays Warhol in Julian Schnabel's* Basquiat	•*J.K. Rowling:* Harry Potter and the Philosopher's Stone
8	•*Peter Davies:* The Hot One Hundred	•*Launch of the Apple iMac in candy colours*	•*Aronofsky's* Pi •*Carrey in* The Truman Show	•*Talvin Singh:* ok •*Louis Sachar:* Holes
9	•*Louise Bourgeois:* Maman	•*Libeskind: Jewish Museum, Berlin*	•*Lucas:* Episode 1: The Phantom Menace	•*Philip Glass:* Dracula

INDEX

abstraction 10–11, 25, 26, 30
AIDS 17, 30
Amore (Koons) 23
'A New Spirit in Painting' exhibition 12
Arroz con Pollo (Basquiat) 16–17
At the Edge of the World (Kapoor) 8, 9

Bad Painting 14–15, 30
Balloon Dog (Koons) 23
Baselitz, Georg 13
Basquiat, Jean-Michel 5, 16–17
Bear (McQueen) 27
Berlin Wall 4, 12, 30
Birnbaum, Dara 26
Bleeding (Gilbert & George) 17
Blood (Jarman) 21
body scarring 21
Bourgeois, Louise 19
Burnished Sky (Riley) 10

Certain Day (Riley) 10
Chadwick, Helen 19
Chia, Sandro 12
Christo & Jeanne-Claude 18
Clemente, Francesco 12
computer art 5, 24, 25, 28–29
Concert for Anarchy (Horn) 18
Cooker, The (Tilson) 28–29
Crack is Wack (Haring) 17
Cucchi, Enzo 12

Daemonization (Salle) 15
Davies, Peter 7
Deadpan (McQueen) 27
diptych 15, 27, 30
drug abuse 17

Electronic Superhighway (Paik) 26, 27
Emin, Tracey 19

ENIAC computer 28
Eurotrash 22
Ever is Over All (Rist) 27
Evolution of Form, The (Latham) 28

Galápagos (Sims) 27
Gamma (Silo) (Wilson Twins) 27
Gates, Bill 5
Gaultier, Jean-Paul 22
Generation X 6
Gilbert & George 17, 24
Graffiti Art 5, 16–17, 30
Gursky, Andreas 25

Haring, Keith 16, 17
Heron, Patrick 10, 11
HIDEO, It's Me, Mama (Idemitsu) 26
High Tech Allergy (Paik) 5, 26
Hirst, Damien 5, 10, 20–21
Hockney, David 11, 25
Holocaust 8, 30
Hong Kong, Grand Hyatt Park (Gursky) 25
Horn, Rebecca 18
Hot One Hundred, The (Davies) 7
House (Whiteread) 8
Humanity Asleep (Schnabel) 15

Idemitsu, Mako 26
I Do Not Know What It Is I Am Like (Viola) 26
Ignorance=Fear (Haring) 17
Impressionism 11, 30
Internet 5, 28–29, 30

Jump (Schnabel) 15

Kapoor, Anish 8–9
Kiefer, Anselm 13
Kitsch Art 22–23, 30
Koons, Jeff 5, 22, 23

Kusama, Yayoi 19

Landers, Sean 6, 7
Latham, William 28
Lichtenstein, Roy 18
Lilith (Kiefer) 13

Maman (Bourgeois) 19
Matisse, Henri 10, 11
McQueen, Steve 27
Minimalism 8–9, 30
Monet, Claude 11
Mori, Mariko 24
Mother and Child Divided (Hirst) 20
Mural with Blue Brush-strokes (Lichtenstein) 18
Muybridge, Eadweard 24

Nauman, Bruce 6, 7, 8
Neo-Expressionism 5, 12–13, 30

Ofili, Chris 20, 21
Oldenburg, Claes 18, 28
One Hundred Live and Die (Nauman) 6

Paik, Nam June 4, 5, 26–27
Paladino, Mimmo 12
Paris, Montparnasse (Gursky) 25
Pearblossom Highway… (Hockney) 25
Performance Art 6, 26, 30
Physical Impossibility of Death in the Mind of Someone Living, The (Hirst) 20–21
Pierre et Gilles 22
Pop Art 11, 18, 19, 30
Popples (Koons) 23
Puppy (Koons) 22

Quinn, Marc 21

Reagan, Ronald 14

Richter, Gerhard 11
Riley, Bridget 10
Rio Videowall (Birnbaum) 26
Rist, Pipilotti 27

St. John (Richter) 11
Salle, David 15
Schnabel, Julian 5, 14, 15, 17
Self (Quinn) 21
Sherman, Cindy 24
Sims, Karl 28
Stasi City (Wilson Twins) 27
Stock Exchange, Tokyo (Gursky) 25
Street (Gilbert & George) 24

Text-Painting (Davies) 7
Tilson, Jake 28–29
Toy Story 5, 29
Transavantgarde 12, 30
Truman Show, The 26

Untitled (Clemente) 12
Untitled (Kapoor) 8
Untitled (Book Corridors) (Whiteread) 8
Untitled #193 (Sherman) 24

van Bruggen, Coosje 18
Video Art 4, 5, 6, 26–27, 30
Viola, Bill 26
vitrine 20, 30

Wall Street 14, 23
When I Am Pregnant (Kapoor) 9
White Anger/Red Danger/Yellow Peril/ Black Death (Nauman) 6
Whiteread, Rachel 8
Wigan, Willard 18
Wilson, Jane & Louise 27